BURIED TO BLOOM

Vanessa Ortiz

ABSOLUTE AUTHOR PUBLISHING HOUSE

Publisher: Absolute Author Publishing House
Editor: Dr. Melissa Caudle
Interior Design: Dr. Melissa Caudle
Cover Design: Rebeca @Fiverr.com

Paperback ISBN: 979-8-89401-088-5
eBook ISBN: 979-8-89401-089-2

pm.   cm.

1.   Spirituality   2. Self-help   3. Women's Motivational

PRINTED IN THE UNITED STATES OF AMERICA

Dedication

To my Heavenly Father, this book is Yours. Every page is a testimony of Your faithfulness, mercy, and power to redeem what was broken. Thank You for never letting go of me, for calling me out of the dirt, and for planting me in purpose. May *Buried to Bloom* bring You glory and draw hearts back to You.

To my son, Yohannes, my oldest, kind, and sweet boy. I pray you grow to mirror the heart of Christ and become the man God created you to be.

To my daughter, Valencia, your joy, strength, and light inspire me daily. May you always know how deeply loved and chosen you are.

To my parents, thank you for planting seeds of faith in me. Your support and encouragement have helped shape who I am today. I honor your legacy.

To my church family, thank you for covering me in prayer, encouraging me through my healing, and walking beside me in every season.

To Pastor Louie, Pastor Eunice, and Pastor Josiah, thank you your leadership, prayers, and prophetic guidance helped me see beyond my pain and step into my purpose. Additionally for believing in the call of God on my life.

To the women who feel buried, this is for you. You are not forgotten. The same God who met me in the dark is ready to breathe life into your story. May you bloom in His timing, rooted in His love.

Author's Note

The Whisper That Birthed the Bloom

I never set out to write a book. Honestly, when people would mention it, I'd laugh. It wasn't something I imagined myself doing. I didn't feel qualified. I didn't think I had the words.

But the Holy Spirit had a different plan.

As time passed and my intimacy with Jesus deepened, especially in the secret place, I began to ask Him:

"Why do You have me here?"

"What are You trying to do in me?"

And each time, I heard the same whisper:

"I'm building seeds of faith."

Those words kept coming, especially when I felt discouraged, confused, or questioned what was happening. He would gently remind me again and again: "I'm building seeds of faith."

It became an anchor. A promise. A prophetic blueprint.

As my faith strengthened, I began to feel a desire to share what God was doing in me, but I didn't know how. I didn't have a platform or a plan. But the whisper returned: "Share the seeds of faith." And that's how this book was birthed.

Not from striving. Not from ambition. But from stillness, surrender, and the soft whisper of a God who plants deep things in hidden places.

Every chapter in *Buried to Bloom* is a seed. Every story is a testimony. Every prayer is a watering of what He's growing in you. So, if you're reading this, know that this isn't just a book—it's a garden of faith, planted with tears and watered by the Word. It was never about me. It's always been about Him.

May the same Holy Spirit who whispered to me whisper to you now. May every buried place in your life begin to bloom.

With love and faith,

Vanessa Ortiz

TABLE OF CONTENTS

Introduction

From Breaking to Blooming: A Seed Story

I remember the night I lay face down on the carpet, the only light in the room illuminating from a hallway I didn't want to walk down. I had just come out of a conversation that left me shattered, carrying the weight of a broken marriage, a crushed identity, and a future I couldn't see. My whispered prayer through the tears was simple, "God, have You forgotten me?"

I felt stripped, emptied, and afraid. But God didn't leave me there.

He met me in the dirt.

This book was born in that place, the hidden space where nothing looked like life, yet something holy was growing beneath the surface. What looked like the end was actually the beginning. What felt like

being buried was, in the Spirit, being planted.
God doesn't waste brokenness, He uses it.

This is more than a collection of words; it's a living
testimony. It's for the woman who feels hidden,
overlooked, or stuck in a season she doesn't
understand. It's for the one who's prayed for a
breakthrough but keeps running into silence. It's for
the seed that's been pressed into the ground, unsure
if it will ever rise.

What breaks you won't bury you. It will plant you.
There's a quote that's stayed with me:

> *"The seed does not ask why it has been*
> *surrounded by darkness. Its only focus is*
> *to reach for the light."* Avellino Farms

And that's what this journey is about: reaching for
the light, even when everything around you feels
like darkness. I realize that the process of growth is
rarely comfortable. It's messy, hidden, and often
misunderstood. But it's never wasted. God is always
at work beneath the surface, shaping us, pruning us,
and preparing us for the promise.

Being planted in good soil isn't just about knowing
God; it's about surrendering to Him, allowing His
Word to take root in your heart, learning to hear His
voice, and trusting Him even when you can't see

what He's doing. It's a life of obedience, intimacy, and faith, rooted in the presence of the One who never stops pursuing you.

Each chapter in this book is rooted in truth, watered by experience, and written with my prayer that it would minister deeply to your spirit. You'll read about seasons of pruning, pain, and surrender, but also purpose, growth, and fruitfulness. Because, in God's hands, the soil is not a place of death; it's the birthplace of destiny.

So, if you're in a season where everything feels stripped away, if your heart feels dry, your spirit weary, and your faith tested, I want you to know you're not alone. This is not the end of your story. You were never buried to be forgotten. You were buried to bloom.

Let's begin this journey together.

BURIED TO BLOOM

Chapter 1

The Seed and the Soil

Faith doesn't begin with blooming. It begins underground, buried, unseen, and pressed beneath the weight of silence.

That is exactly where I found myself during one of the hardest seasons of my life.

I didn't know it then, but God was tilling the soil of my heart, breaking things open so something new could begin.

It was painful, lonely, and hidden. But it was also holy.

I had checked all the boxes. I had dreams, a plan, and what I thought was the right path. But the soil I had planted my life in wasn't what God had chosen for me; it was what I had chosen for myself, out of pressure, out of fear, and out of the need to move forward.

Eventually, that soil, no matter how good it looked on the surface, began to reveal its lack of depth. The relationship I thought would bring life only brought loss.

The path I thought would lead to purpose only led to pain.

And still, God was there. In the dark. In the dirt. In the place that looked like the end.

When You Plant Without God

I didn't always understand the danger of planting outside of God's will. Sometimes we step into things prematurely, with good intentions, but in the wrong soil. When the storms come, the roots cannot hold. That is where I found myself: heartbroken, confused, and stripped of everything I thought was permanent.

But God wasn't punishing me. He was rescuing me. He was lovingly uprooting me from toxic soil and replanting me in a space where I could actually grow.

It wasn't easy. The breaking hurt. I questioned my worth, my future, and even my identity. But in that breaking, God showed me something deeper.

Faith Is a Seed. Surrender Is the Soil.

In the Parable of the Sower (*Luke 8:5–15*), Jesus teaches that the seed—the Word of God—is always good. Whether it grows depends on the soil of the heart.

Some seed falls on the path—snatched away before it can take root.

Some falls on rocky ground—it sprouts quickly, but dies when pressure comes.

Some falls among thorns—choked by distractions and worries. But some fall on good soil—produces a multiplied harvest. I had to ask myself: *What kind of soil am I?*

There were seasons when my heart was stony, hearing God's Word but resisting its depth. Pride, unforgiveness, and sin kept it from taking root. But God is so patient. His mercy softens hard places.

> *"I will give you a new heart and put a new spirit in you; I will remove from you your heart of stone and give you a heart of flesh." Ezekiel 36:26*

3

Even when we resist Him, He continues to pursue us, offering healing and transformation. Do not harden your heart. Let God break up the soil and prepare it for His Word.

There were also seasons when I was caught in thorny soil: distracted, overwhelmed, trying to follow Christ, but still entangled in worldly attachments or emotionally draining relationships. The longer I tried to settle into something that was not God-ordained, the more disoriented I became.

> *"But the worries of this life, the deceitfulness of wealth, and the desires for other things come in and choke the word, making it unfruitful." Mark 4:19*

These thorns choke out growth. And sometimes they are subtle—busyness, striving, even good things that crowd out God things. We have to do heart checks often and clear the soil.

Good Soil: Where Faith Grows Deep

> *"But the seed falling on good soil refers to someone who hears the word and understands it." Matthew 13:23*

Good soil is a surrendered heart: humble, soft, and ready to obey. When the seed lands there, it grows. It

4

produces fruit that remains. You walk in a peace that surpasses understanding, a strength that is not your own.

As my posture shifted into good soil, everything changed. I became receptive. I was able to hear and move. I was grounded in truth, not emotion. God became my anchor, not the opinions of others.

There is a supernatural force that moves through surrendered soil, a divine pull that keeps you rooted in Christ no matter what comes. When you are planted in Him, your life produces fruit. Not because you strive, but because He is the Vine and you are the branch.

> *"And some fell into good soil, and grew up and produced a crop a hundred times as great." Luke 8:8*

Where You Plant Yourself Shapes Everything

Where your spirit is rooted determines where your life will grow. If you are struggling with cycles, you cannot seem to break, it is time to ask, What soil am I in?

Are you planted in God's truth, or in performance, pressure, and self-reliance?

Are you nourishing your faith with the Word, or feeding your fear with the noise around you?

Jesus taught in parables for a reason. He wanted those who were truly hungry to press in and receive deeper truth. The soil of the heart matters more than anything else.

> *"To you it has been given to know the mysteries of the kingdom of heaven..."*
> *Matthew 13:11*

You cannot grow if you do not surrender.

The Anatomy of a Seed

A seed is small, silent, and hidden.

And yet, inside of it is everything needed to become what it was created to be.

But first, it must break.

The shell must crack. The inside must be exposed. That breaking is not the end; it is the beginning of life. And it is the same with us.

God uses pressure seasons to break through our pride and reveal purpose. He allows the dark places to do their work. In the silence, He speaks. In the dirt, He forms new life.

The Breaking That Brought Me Back to Life

My "buried season" was filled with stripping and surrender. I walked through disappointment, isolation, abuse, and the pain of becoming a single mother. I fought battles I didn't have the language for at the time.

But through it all, God was with me.

He used that soil to teach me to hear His voice. He used the silence to teach me to worship.

He used the breaking to root me in His truth.

I began to choose worship over worry, truth over trauma, and faith, even when I couldn't see the fruit.

Check Your Soil

If you feel buried right now, let me ask: What kind of soil are you in?

Are you rooted in Christ, or your own understanding?

Are you surrendering your plans, or clinging to what God is asking you to release?

Are you allowing His Word to take root, or just skimming the surface?

Some darkness is divine. Some silence is sacred. It is not always the enemy; sometimes, it is God covering you in stillness so He can reshape your heart.

Ask Him:

> *"Lord, am I buried in good soil, or are You calling me to be replanted?"*

Let the Seed Break

I am not here because I got it all right. I am here because I finally let the seed break. I surrendered my will. I gave up control. I allowed God to crack open the shell I had built around myself, and that is where life began.

So do not despise the dirt. Do not fear the breaking. Because that is where blooming begins.

Reflection Questions

What soil have I been planted in—God's will or my

comfort?

What part of my heart is God asking to break open so new life can grow?
In what areas of my life have I confused burial with planting?

Prayer Prompt

Father,

Thank You for meeting me in the soil. Even when I do not understand the darkness, I trust that You are doing something deep beneath the surface. Break the parts of me that need breaking: my pride, my fear, my self-will. Replant me in good soil, rooted in Your Word and surrendered to Your will. I choose to believe this is not the end; it is the beginning of something beautiful.

In Jesus' name, amen.

Chapter 2

Hidden But Growing –
Faith in the Dark
Seasons

Sometimes, God grows us in the dark.

Not in the spotlight.

Not in the applause.

Not on the platform.

But in the secret, quiet, often painful places where no one else sees.

It is easy to confuse hiddenness with being overlooked.

It is easy to think God has forgotten you when it feels like nothing is happening.

However, I have learned that the most powerful growth happens underground.

The Hidden Place Is Holy Ground

When a seed is planted, it does not bloom overnight. It sits buried in the soil, surrounded by silence. There are no signs of life. No movement. No fruit.

But deep beneath the surface, something sacred happens.

Roots form. Foundations laid. Identity is taking shape long before anyone sees the bloom.

That is how faith grows in dark seasons. God often hides us to protect us, to develop us, and to make sure that when we rise, we rise in Him, not in striving, not in shallow soil, and not in pride, but fully rooted in truth.

I used to think hiddenness meant I was being punished, that I had missed my opportunity, perhaps maybe I was not enough. But now I see it clearly: the hidden place is where identity is formed.

Faith Doesn't Skip the Process

There was a season when everything in my life felt quiet. God had just brought me through the most painful storm I had ever experienced. I was grieving at what I thought my life would look like. As a single mother, I was walking through new responsibilities, unfamiliar spiritual warfare, and a lot of unknowns. I kept praying, "God, what are You doing?"

I did not realize that in the silence; He was growing me.

I was not being punished.

I was being prepared.

I was not delayed.

I was being developed.

I was not forgotten.

I was being rooted.

This chapter of my journey was not loud. It was not full of open doors or dramatic moments. But it was holy. And it was in the quiet where my relationship with Jesus deepened in a way it never had before.

When You Feel Like Nothing Is Happening

I want to speak to the woman who feels like she is doing everything right, but still sees no fruit.
You are praying.

You are showing up.

You are being obedient.

But everything still feels stuck.

Let me remind you: Just because you are hidden does not mean you are not growing.

Just because you do not see fruit yet does not mean your roots are not going deep.

Just because it is silent does not mean God is absent. Some seasons are not about doing.

They are about becoming.

He's Growing You in the Dark

God is building something in you that cannot be rushed. What may feel like isolation is actually intimacy.

What may feel like delay is actually development.

He is teaching you to hear His voice, to depend on His Word, and to worship when no one is watching.

He is growing something within you so that when the doors open, you will not forget who opened them.

In this hidden season, I learned how to rest. I learned that being unseen by people does not mean I am unseen by God.

 I learned that fruit grows in its time, but roots grow now.

Don't Rush the Rise

It is tempting to want to arrive, to seek visibility, and to desire the bloom without the burial. But if you rise too soon, without roots, you will topple when the wind comes.

God does not just want you to be seen; He wants you to be sustained.

And the only way to sustain what He is building is to stay in the soil until He says it is time.

To the One in Hiding

If you are in a hidden season, let this be your encouragement:
Stay faithful.

Stay rooted.

Stay surrendered.

Even if no one else sees it, God sees the seed.
And when the time is right, He will make it bloom.

Reflection Questions

Have I mistaken God's hiddenness for His absence?

How has He been working in the silence?

What roots is God developing in me right now, even if no one else sees them?

What might God be protecting me from by keeping me hidden in this season?

Prayer Prompt

Lord,

Thank You for the hidden seasons. Even when I feel

invisible, I believe You are growing something deep inside me. Help me to rest in Your timing and to trust that my roots are being established for the fruit You have planned. When it feels like nothing is happening, remind me that You do Your best work in the unseen. I surrender my desire for visibility and choose to abide in You.

In Jesus' name, amen.

Chapter 3

Planted for Purpose

Pruning, Pain & Preparation

God does not waste pain. He repurposes it. There is purpose in the pruning, and there is preparation in the pain.

What feels like loss is often divine alignment.

Pruning Isn't Punishment—It's Protection

> *"I am the true vine, and my Father is the gardener. He cuts off every branch in me that bears no fruit, while every branch that does bear fruit he prunes so that it will be even more fruitful." John 15:1–2 (NIV)*

That verse wrecked me in the best way. Because I was bearing fruit, I was walking with God.

I had said yes. Despite that, things began to fall away: relationships, roles, responsibilities I thought I was called to carry.

I was confused. God, did I not do what You asked?

But the answer was not, "You failed."

It was, "You are being pruned for greater."

Sometimes what looks like loss is really God trimming what cannot carry the weight of your next season.

The Flowers That Needed Space

During one of the loneliest seasons of my life, God spoke to me through a simple bouquet.

I had been crying out, "Why am I so alone? Why does it feel like everyone is being stripped away?

That day, I looked at the bouquet beside me. Each flower had bloomed beautifully, and God whispered:

"They only bloomed because they had space. If they were too crowded, they could not open up the way I designed them to."

Then He said:

"That is what I am doing with you. I am making room for you to bloom."

What I saw as isolation was actually intention. What felt like loneliness was really love.

He's Not Punishing You—He's Protecting the Fruit

When God begins to cut, it can feel as though you're losing everything. The process is painful and disorienting. But often, what He is really doing is removing what isn't rooted in Him, what has been hindering your growth and blocking your bloom.
For me, part of that pruning came through a kind of pain I never saw coming.

I endured deep emotional, mental, and spiritual abuse in my marriage. It didn't look like abuse at first. In the beginning, the signs were subtle. But over time, the manipulation became more intense and harder to ignore.

Slowly, I began to lose myself, caught in a cycle of confusion, shame, and silence.

I remember planning a surprise party, filled with love and excitement, only to be met with coldness and criticism. My efforts were dismissed. My presence never seemed to be enough. Again and again, I was made to feel small, overlooked, and diminished.

The more I pressed into God, the more resistance I encountered at home. It seemed that the deeper I pursued Him, the more hostility I faced.

I will never forget the moment the illusion shattered. I was sitting quietly, reading the book of *Romans*, when his words cut through the stillness like a knife: "You have changed. I do not even recognize you."

He was right. Something in me had changed, something irreversible. Without even realizing it, my heart had been shifting day by day as I surrendered more of myself to Christ. Now, the evidence of that transformation could no longer be hidden.

At that moment, I understood something profound. Not that I had become someone unfamiliar to myself. It was that I had finally become who I was always meant to be covered, protected, and known.

I was no longer weighed down by human expectations, but securely under the authority of Christ.

The deeper I stepped into God's light, the more the darkness around me resisted. I fought hard to stay.

I prayed for change, believed for healing, and clung to hope far longer than wisdom would have advised.

But in His mercy, God whispered a truth to my spirit, a truth that set me free:

"You cannot grow in poisoned soil."

Leaving was not giving up. It was answering the call to live.

It meant trusting that sometimes the greatest act of faith is not staying in what is familiar, but stepping into the unknown, where God can plant you in soil prepared for your flourishing.

When Walking Away Is the Bravest Way to Walk Toward Him

The day I surrendered was not the day I gave up. It

was the day I made a conscious choice to start living differently. I chose to step toward healing, to create a safe and nurturing environment for my children, and to allow God to replant me in soil that could truly support life.

What once felt like failure began to reveal itself as the first step toward freedom.

Laying it All Down

God asked me to lay down more than just the relationship. He also asked me to surrender my timeline, my idea of what a calling should look like, and the version of life and identity I had built for myself.

Each time I said "yes" to Him, it felt like something in me was dying. But with every surrender, I found myself drawing closer to the purpose He had prepared for me.

> *"Whoever wants to save their life will lose it, but whoever loses their life for me will find it." Matthew 16:25 (NIV)*

I had to learn to trust the Gardener, even when my hands were bleeding from the loss. He knew what needed to be removed in order for me to grow, even when I didn't understand it at the time.

22

Preparation Feels Like Breaking

One night, through tears, I cried out, "God, why does this hurt so much?" And in the quiet, He answered:

"Because I am preparing you to carry more."
The breaking wasn't without purpose. It was divine. It was the process of crushing pride, removing idols, and stripping away everything in my life that wasn't rooted in Him

.

> *"Consider it pure joy... whenever you face trials... because you know that the testing of your faith produces perseverance."* James 1:2–3 (NIV)

Purpose Is Often Revealed in the Wilderness

It's a biblical pattern:

Moses was called, then spent 40 years in the desert. David was anointed, then ran for his life before becoming King. Jesus was led into the wilderness before His ministry began.

> *"Then Jesus was led by the Spirit into the wilderness to be tempted..."* Matthew 4:1 (NIV)

The wilderness is not a form of punishment; it is a place of preparation. It is where your identity is refined, where the noise of the world fades, and where God's voice becomes clear and unmistakable.

Let the Pain Do Its Work

Maybe right now you are in a place of grief, transition, or uncertainty. Maybe your obedience still led you into heartbreak.

Let me tell you this: the pain has a purpose. The pruning is making room for fruit. The preparation is positioning you for your next assignment.

> *"And we know that in all things God works for the good of those who love him..." Romans 8:28 (NIV)*

Let the tears water the ground. Allow the roots to grow deep. God is planting you for something greater.

You're Being Made Ready

There is a strength that can only be forged in fire, the kind comfort will never produce. There is a wisdom that forms in the waiting, in a way that speed can never replicate. And there is a depth shaped in the dark, the kind the spotlight will never teach.

"Humble yourselves, therefore, under God's mighty hand, that He may lift you up in due time." 1 Peter 5:6 (NIV)

You are not behind. You are not broken beyond repair. You are not forgotten. You are being made ready. So, lean into the pruning, yield to the process, and trust that even in the pain, God is preparing you for purpose.

Reflection Questions

What has God been pruning in my life—and have I been resisting or releasing it?
How is my current pain preparing me for future purpose?

Can I look back and see how past "losses" were actually God's protection or redirection?

Prayer Prompt

Jesus,

I trust You as the Gardener of my life. I may not understand the cutting, but I choose to believe that every pruning is preparing me to carry more of Your glory.

Help me to let go of what no longer serves Your purpose. Let my pain become preparation. Grow my faith in the wilderness, and teach me to see purpose where I once saw only loss. I yield to the process.

In Your name, amen.

Chapter 4

Obedience – The Soil of Surrender

Obedience is the bridge between the seed and the bloom. It is the space where faith turns into action, where the Word takes root and begins to shape who we are.

But here's what I have learned: obedience does not always feel good, it does not always make sense, and it rarely comes without cost.

Surrender Is the True Soil of Growth

When God called me to obey in deeply personal areas such as my relationships, identity, and future, I wrestled.

I thought I had surrendered, but obedience revealed the parts of my heart I was still trying to control.

"If you are willing and obedient, you shall eat the good of the land." Isaiah 1:19 (NKJV)

That verse became an anchor. Even when obedience led me into uncertainty, I held onto this truth: God's plans are always better than mine, even when they hurt.

Partial Obedience Is Still Disobedience

There were moments I wanted to negotiate with God:

"Okay, Lord, I will let go of this relationship, but can I keep this connection just in case?"

"Okay, God, I will say yes to ministry, but only if it looks like this."

But the Holy Spirit gently reminded me: Obedience is not on your terms. It is on His.

"Trust in the Lord with all your heart and lean not on your own understanding; in all your ways submit to Him, and He will make your paths straight." Proverbs 3:5–6 (NIV)

I had to stop leaning on what made sense and start stepping where He called, even if it looked like wilderness. Even if it looked like less. Even if it cost me everything I thought I needed.

There Is Glory on the Other Side of Obedience
Each time I obeyed, even through fear and even through tears, God met me with peace.
It did not always get easier, but I became stronger.
My spirit aligned. My vision sharpened. My identity solidified.

> *"Blessed rather are those who hear the word of God and obey it." Luke 11:28 (NIV)*

Obedience did not erase the pain, but it gave the pain purpose.

It turned my valleys into vineyards, my wilderness into worship, my silence into sacred intimacy with the One who speaks beyond words.

Surrendering the Outcome

One of the hardest things God asked me to surrender was how He would work things out. I wanted control. I wanted a timeline. I wanted certainty. But He wanted my heart.

"Your word is a lamp to my feet and a light to my path." Psalm 119:105 (ESV)

Not a spotlight. Not a floodlight. A lamp. One step at a time.

Obedience meant walking without all the answers. It meant trusting that each "yes" was planting something eternal, even when I could not see the bloom yet.

Obedience Will Cost You Something—But it Will Give You More

It cost me comfort.

It cost me relationships.

It cost me the version of life I had built on my own. But in return?

It gave me purpose. It gave me peace.

It gave me presence—the kind that only comes when you walk closely with God.

"Whoever wants to be My disciple must deny themselves and take up their cross daily and follow Me." Luke 9:23 (NIV)

Obedience is the daily yes. The quiet yes. The sacrificial yes.

It is saying, "Not my will, but Yours be done," even when your heart is still healing and your hands are still trembling.

Stay in the Soil of Surrender

If God is asking you to do something hard, something that does not make sense, do not pull away.

Stay planted.

Stay surrendered. Stay obedient.

Your obedience is watering the seed.

Your "yes" is preparing the way for a breakthrough. And what feels like a small act of faith is actually a powerful act of warfare in the Spirit.

He sees your surrender.

He honors your yes.

And He will bring a harvest from it.

Reflection Questions

What is God asking me to obey that still feels uncomfortable or unclear?

Have I been negotiating with God instead of fully surrendering?

How can I lean into obedience even when I don't have all the answers?

Prayer Prompt

Father,

Help me to trust You fully. Even when obedience feels costly, remind me that You are faithful to bring fruit from every surrendered yes.

I do not want to obey on my terms; I want to yield completely. Give me the courage to say yes, even when it stretches me. Root me in Your will, and lead me step by step into the harvest You have prepared.

In Jesus' name, amen.

Chapter 4.5

When God Speaks in the Soil – Discerning His Voice in the Dark

There is a kind of silence that does not signal absence; it invites intimacy. I used to think God's voice only came through thunder, that it would always be loud, clear, and unmistakable. In the quiet moments of my life, especially when I was surrounded by uncertainty and pain,

I slowly recognized the gentle, steady whisper of God. It did not come through noise or dramatic signs, but through His quiet presence. This chapter is for the woman who is asking, "God, how do I know it is You?"

In breaking seasons, every voice can feel loud: fear, doubt, pressure, opinions. The soil can be confusing, and it is also where the Voice of God becomes most precious.

A Whisper That Anchors

During one of my darkest nights, I cried out, "God, what now?"

I didn't hear an audible response, but a single word settled deep in my spirit: **Trust.**

It wasn't dramatic or emotional. It was steady. It was rooted.

That is the nature of His voice. It does not stir emotion; it plants something solid in the soil of your soul.

> *"My sheep hear My voice, and I know them, and they follow Me." John 10:27 (ESV)*

What God's Voice Sounds Like

God's voice is: Consistent with Scripture. He never contradicts His Word.

Peace-filled, even in correction – Conviction brings clarity, not confusion.

34

Persistent – His whispers return again and again.

Personal – His voice sounds like a relationship, not a religion.

If what you are hearing causes panic, anxiety, or condemnation, it is not Him.

Yes, He may call you to difficult things.

He never shames you.

He calls you forward in love.

Ways God Speaks in the Soil

- Through His Word – Scripture becomes alive, as if it's reading you.

- Through Stillness – When you finally stop striving, His whisper becomes clear.

- Through Confirmation – Repeated words, scriptures, or prophetic insight from others.

- Through Dreams or Visions – Often during deep rest or surrender.

- Through Peace – Not the absence of hardship, but a supernatural stillness within.

Sometimes it is a verse that will not leave your heart.

Sometimes it is a vision that calms your spirit.

Sometimes it is silence, yet even then, your soul knows He is near.

Learning to Discern His Whisper

You do not learn God's voice by striving. You learn it by sitting.

The more time you spend in His presence, the more clearly you will recognize what is and is not Him. It is like learning a melody. You may not catch every note at first, but over time, it becomes familiar.

> *"Be still, and know that I am God." Psalm 46:10 (NIV)*

Stillness sharpens spiritual hearing.

When you're planted in a season of stillness, God is not rushing to fix things. He is drawing you deeper into trust.

What If I Don't Hear Anything?

Sometimes God is silent on the outside because He is speaking on the inside.

He may not be saying anything new because He has already spoken. He is waiting for you to move on with the last word. Or maybe the silence is an invitation: to seek Him, not just His answers.
Silence does not mean abandonment. Sometimes silence is confirmation: Stay planted. Stay faithful. Stay still.

Practical Ways to Discern His Voice

- Create quiet space daily – No phone. No pressure. Just stillness.

- Ask and wait – "Lord, what are You saying
- today?"

- Write what you sense – Journaling creates space for clarity and flow.

- Test it – Does it align with scripture? Does it bring peace?

- Submit it – Bring what you hear to trusted mentors or leaders.

You will not always get it perfect. But God is not looking for perfection; He is looking for pursuit. Trust in Him and when your heart is surrendered, He will make Himself known.

Reflection Questions

How has God spoken to me in past seasons— what did His voice feel like?

What distractions might be drowning out His whisper right now?

Am I seeking clarity more than I'm seeking closeness?

Prayer Prompt

Father,

Teach me to know Your voice. In the stillness, speak. In the soil, plant truth that anchors me in Your presence. I surrender the noise, the pressure, and the need to figure it all out. I just want You. Help me discern the difference between fear and faith, emotion and instruction. Let Your Word guide me.

Let Your Spirit lead me. Let Your whisper become the loudest sound in my life.

In Jesus' name, amen.

Chapter 4.6

Soaking in His Presence – Meditating on the Word and Hearing His Voice

There is a stillness that transforms you. A stillness where your spirit meets the Spirit of God, with no striving, no performing, just being. This is what it means to soak in His presence.

It's Not a Formula—It's Fellowship

Soaking is not about checking a spiritual box. It is not something to master; it is something to enter.

It is a posture of intimacy, a space where your soul breathes again.

It is sitting with the One who created you and letting

His Word wash over you until His voice becomes the loudest sound in your life.

Meditation: Biblical, Not Borrowed

When people hear "meditation," they often think of clearing the mind or centering the self. But biblical meditation is not about emptiness; it is about fullness.

It is filling your heart with truth.

It is reflecting on God's Word until it takes root.

It is letting Scripture become your anchor, your mirror, and your compass.

> *"But his delight is in the law of the Lord, and on his law he meditates day and night." Psalm 1:2 (ESV)*

Meditation is dwelling. It is staying long enough with one verse until it becomes a revelation.

Try this:

Read one Scripture slowly, out loud if needed.
Ask, "God, what are You saying to me through this?"

Let it lead you into deeper communion.

Soaking: The Posture of Stillness

Soaking is exactly what it sounds like: lingering in the presence of God. It is not a rushed devotional or a checklist of prayers.

It is simply being still, surrendered, and open. It means turning down the noise, laying everything at His feet, and saying:

"I am here, Jesus. I just want You."

You do not need fancy words.

You do not have to feel anything immediately.

You just need willingness, a soft heart, and a still spirit.

The Soaking That Saved Me

I will never forget the first time I truly experienced soaking in God's presence.

I was broken, exhausted, and desperate for God to intervene.
A new mother, only three months postpartum, barely

functioning. I was fighting for my marriage, praying daily, pressing into Scripture, but the pain only grew.

The abuse deepened. I was clinging to God, but I was also drowning.

Then one night, I attended a healing prayer service, a soaking session.

I walked in with nothing left but hope. The worship was soft, the lights dim, and something inside me finally gave way. I stopped pretending to be okay. I sat quietly and let the tears fall.

In that stillness, something holy began to happen. God spoke, not through thunder or noise, but through His presence.

He spoke through comfort, through peace, and through the quiet assurance that He was near. I felt Him wrap me in His love.

I knew, really knew, that He saw me. That He had not forgotten me. That He was holding me in the storm.

And then, I had a vision.

The Vision That Changed Everything

In this vision, I saw myself holding a small teddy bear. Jesus stood before me, extending His hand, asking me to give it to Him. I resisted. I clutched it tightly.

That bear symbolized everything I was afraid to lose: my marriage, my expectations, my control.

Then I saw what was behind His back. It was a much bigger teddy bear, something better, something greater, but I could not receive it until I was willing to let go. That vision broke me open. Tears flowed as I wrestled with surrender. Toward the end of the session, I released it. I let go of the pain, the striving, and the fear.

In that moment, something supernatural happened. God healed my heart.

His presence flooded me. Years of grief lifted.

Years of prayers met with one sacred moment of surrender. I left that service changed.

I no longer knew God as Healer only in theory. I knew Him as Healer in my own story.

From that day forward, He began restoring me

emotionally, spiritually, and even physically.

And it all began in stillness.

You Can't Hear in the Noise if You don't listen.

Don't Make Space for the Whisper

Soaking is where your roots grow deep. It is the place where lies begin to lose their grip and where healing becomes personal.

> *"Be still, and know that I am God." Psalm 46:10 (NIV)*

In the stillness, you are not being ignored; you are being known. You are not forgotten; you are being formed.

You Don't Have to Strive to Hear Him

Soaking teaches us that God speaks more through His presence than through our performance. You do not have to beg. You do not have to strive. You simply have to rest.

During a quiet season of seeking God, I had a dream that forever marked me.

45

I did not fully understand it at first, but over time, the Holy Spirit began to reveal the depths of what I saw and felt.

What follows is the journal entry I wrote after that dream, shared here in hopes that it will stir your spirit too.

The Glory That Rests

During a quiet season of seeking God, I had a dream that forever marked me.

I did not fully understand it at first, but over time, the Holy Spirit began to reveal the depths of what I saw and felt.

Dream Journal Entry

Love Wrapped in Wings

There are moments when God doesn't need to speak audibly; He simply makes His presence known. This was one of those moments.

In my dream, I was lying in bed when I suddenly became aware that I wasn't alone. To my right, a majestic, lion-like being was lying beside me, aligned horizontally, just as I was.

At first, it faced forward, calm and present. But when it sensed that I had become aware of its presence, it slowly turned its head and looked directly at me.

The moment our eyes met, I was completely undone. The being had wings, expansive and glowing with golden light, and its form radiated strength and peace. Its face was unlike anything I had ever seen.

It held the mystery of the cherubim described in Ezekiel's vision: four distinct faces, a lion, an ox, an eagle, and a man.

Each one carried part of God's nature: His authority, endurance, vision, and compassion.

Even though it didn't speak, its gaze said everything. It was loving, watchful, and fiercely peaceful.

All around us, light flowed, warm, golden, and alive. The atmosphere was charged with the presence of God, yet completely still. Sacred.

I wasn't afraid. I was seen. Fully known. Deeply protected.

What I Felt:

- The gaze of Heaven
- Holy stillness
- Tender protection
- Peaceful safety
- Deep love without a word

What I Believe God Was Saying:

> "You are not alone. Even in rest, My glory remains beside you. I have assigned My presence to watch over you. I do not just visit; I stay. You are seen. You are guarded. You are Mine."

This dream wasn't just a moment of comfort; it was a spiritual marker.

It was a moment when God allowed me to witness how completely I am covered by Him, even when I am still.

The cherubim did not need to roar or shine brightly to prove its power. Its stillness was the power. Its gaze was the message.

This was more than protection; it was a visual expression of divine nearness. It reminded me that in the moments when I feel forgotten, overlooked, or unseen, God has already sent heaven to lie beside me.

A Prayer

Lord, thank You for the way You reveal Yourself so gently and so powerfully. Thank You for assigning Your presence to rest with me. Teach me to live from this peace. Open my eyes to recognize Your nearness, even in silence. Let others encounter this kind of love through me.

In Jesus' name, amen.

***

I wasn't alone in the night. His glory was beside me, and His love surrounded me like wings.

"I lay down and slept; I woke again, for the Lord sustained me." Psalm 3:5

Sometimes, He speaks through Scripture.

Sometimes, through a picture or a moment of peace. Other times, through a vision. But always, He speaks in love.

Dream Journal Entry: The Cross in the Corner

This dream came during a sacred time: a seven-day fast where I was seeking God with all my heart, asking Him for clarity, direction, and a deeper encounter. On the seventh day, I woke at 1:11 a.m. with a dream that marked me.

In the dream, I found myself walking the hallway of a school building. The walls were blank, beige, and unremarkable, almost sterile. My spirit knew this place held purpose. I felt a holy prompting to create something on the wall, a prophetic act.

So, I reached up and drew a cross in the upper right-hand corner of the wall. As I traced it, I began to decorate the cross with dark pink flowers, bold, deep, and full of beauty. These flowers weren't just artistic; they felt sacred. They represented new life, healing, and resurrection power.

50

The cross became an altar, right there in an everyday place. Then something unexpected happened. My high school history teacher appeared. He stood nearby and noticed what I was doing.

He didn't interrupt; he simply acknowledged it. In the dream, I remember thinking, *Why him? Why now?*

But his presence felt significant, like a witness. It felt like someone from my past was being allowed to see what God was doing in me now. And then I woke up. At exactly 1:11 a.m.

What I Believe God Was Saying:

> "You're marking spaces with My presence, ordinary places with eternal purpose. The Cross is not just your covering; it is your assignment. I am planting beauty where others see blankness. And I am allowing your past to witness your bloom."

That hallway represented the places God is calling me to carry His presence—places that seem plain or forgotten but are ripe for resurrection.

The flowers represented the bloom that follows the breaking.

And the history teacher symbolized my past, not forgotten but now redeemed. God was showing me that even parts of my life I thought were disconnected or random are being woven into this story of faith. He is allowing the former version of me—the student, the daughter, the one in hiding—to witness what He has grown.

Reflection

That dream reminded me that the Cross is not just something we wear; it is something we plant. It is something we place with intention and carry into every environment we enter. This includes a fast, a hallway, or even a dream. When we choose to bring the Cross with us, God decorates what we dedicate. He causes things to bloom where we choose to obey.

What a Soaking Session Might Look Like

If you've never soaked before, here's a gentle rhythm to follow:

- Set the Atmosphere
- Find a quiet place.
- Play instrumental or soaking worship music.

- Light a candle or dim the lights if that helps you focus.

Center on the Word

- Choose one Scripture. Read it slowly. Ask, "Holy Spirit, what are You saying to me through this?"

Invite His Presence

- Pray simply: "Jesus, I welcome You. I want to hear You. I want to know You."

Be Still

- Lay down, sit, or kneel.

- Close your eyes and breathe deeply.

- Let go of distractions. If your thoughts wander, gently return to the Scripture or to His name.

Listen and Linger

- Don't rush. You might hear a phrase, see a

picture, or feel peace— or you might feel nothing at all. That's okay.

- Journal whatever rises in your spirit.

Reflection Questions

Have I created space in my life to simply be with Jesus, without an agenda?

What scriptures stir something in my spirit when I sit with them?

How can I build a regular rhythm of soaking and stillness?

Prayer Prompt

Jesus,

I want to know You, not just with my mind but with my spirit. Teach me how to slow down and soak in Your presence. Quiet the noise within me and around me.

Let Your Word come alive in my heart, and let Your voice be the sound that shapes me.

I surrender striving. I release fear. I just want You.

Draw me close in the stillness, and let our time together transform me.

*In Your name I rest, **amen.***

Chapter 5

Walking in the Word –
Rooted and Equipped

If faith is the seed and surrender is the soil, then the Word of God is the water. Without it, growth is impossible. We cannot bloom if we are not rooted, and we cannot be rooted if we are not in the Word.

You Can't Walk in Power Without the Word

The Word of God is not optional. It is not a suggestion. It is our sword, our shield, our strength, and our sustenance.

> *"For the word of God is alive and active. Sharper than any double-edged sword..." Hebrews 4:12 (NIV)*

The enemy does not care how emotional you get; he cares how rooted you are. Emotions fade.

But the Word endures, *"Heaven and earth will pass away, but My words will never pass away." Matthew 24:35 (NIV)*

I have walked through warfare that I would not have survived if I did not know the Word. I have faced deception, exhaustion, and spiritual attacks. The only thing that kept me grounded was truth.

Not hype. Not opinions. **Scripture.**

The Word Is a Weapon—Use It

Jesus, the Word made flesh, modeled how to fight the enemy by using the written Word.

In the wilderness, Satan tempted Him, twisted Scripture, and came at Him from every angle. But Jesus did not argue emotionally. He responded by saying: *"It is written..."*

We cannot fight lies if we do not know truth.

We cannot walk in authority if we do not walk in the Word.

You do not need perfect theology. You just need to open the *Book*. Even one verse, meditated on deeply, can transform your mind and strengthen your spirit.

Walking the Word Is More Than Reading It

Don't just read the Bible. Walk it out.

Let it shape your decisions.

Let it confront your flesh. Let it guide your relationships, your boundaries, and your identity.

> *"Your word is a lamp to my feet and a light to my path." Psalm 119:105 (ESV)*

This is not about head knowledge. It is about heart transformation.

God's Word will:

- Renew your mind.
- Heal your identity.
- Expose lies.
- Strengthen your discernment.
- Confirm your calling.

Rooted Women Don't Get Uprooted Easily

When you are rooted in truth:

- You won't fall for flattering lies.

- You won't be shaken by criticism.

- You won't confuse distraction with direction.

- Your roots go deep enough to outlast the storm.

That is how God wants us to live: anchored in His Word and not tossed by the wind.

> *"Then we will no longer be infants, tossed back and forth by the waves, and blown here and there by every wind of teaching..." Ephesians 4:14 (NIV)*

Equipped for Battle, Not Just Blessing

God doesn't give us the Word just to make us feel better. He gives it to equip us.

- You are in a battle.

- You need armor.

- You need weapons.

"Put on the full armor of God, so that you can take your stand against the devil's schemes." Ephesians 6:11 (NIV)

The sword of the Spirit is the Word (*Ephesians 6:17*). And you do not learn to use it by watching someone else swing it. You learn by picking it up for yourself.

You do not have to be perfect to be powerful. You just have to be rooted.

This Word Will Equip You to Raise Others

As I became rooted in the Word, God began to raise me up, not only for my own healing but also to help others grow.

This is the season where God is equipping women to walk in the Word boldly:

- Not to just know scripture, but to teach it.

- Not to just quote truth, but to carry it.

- Not to just study the Word, but to live it. And when you live it, it multiplies.

Reflection Questions

Do I treat the Word like my foundation—or just a supplement?

When was the last time I let a verse confront and transform me?

Am I walking in the Word daily—or only visiting when things go wrong?

Prayer Prompt

Father,

Let Your Word be the foundation of my life. Teach me to love it, crave it, and walk it out. Show me how to wield it as a weapon and receive it as a healing balm.

Plant it deep in my heart so I do not waver in the storm. Help me grow into a woman who is rooted, equipped, and unshakable because Your truth has shaped me.

In Jesus' name, amen.

Chapter 6

The Harvest – Bearing Fruit for His Glory

This is the season you've been sowing for; the season where what was planted in pain begins to bear fruit. It is where what was hidden in darkness rises into the light, and where roots begin to produce results, not for your glory but for His.

> *"Those who sow with tears will reap with songs of joy." Psalm 126:5 (NIV)*

Fruit Comes After the Breaking

You cannot bear fruit if you skip the process. First comes the seed, then the soil. After that comes the stretching, the silence, the surrender, and the breaking.

And only then comes the bloom.

The Fruit Is Not for You Alone

One of the biggest shifts in my life was realizing this: the harvest isn't just about me.

It's about the lives connected to my obedience.

The people who will taste the fruit of my surrender.

The healing that flows through what I allowed God to grow in secret.

> *"This is to my Father's glory, that you bear much fruit, showing yourselves to be my disciples." John 15:8 (NIV)*

God doesn't grow fruit so you can admire yourself. He grows it so you can nourish others.

Your story is someone else's breakthrough. Your "yes" is someone else's rescue.

Your testimony is someone else's map out of the dark.

The Fruit Reveals the Root

Jesus said we would know a tree by its fruit.

"A good tree can't produce bad fruit, and a bad tree can't produce good fruit."
Matthew 7:18 (NLT)

The fruit of your life reveals what has been happening underground. If bitterness is coming out, you have to ask—what has been feeding your roots?

If peace is overflowing, it means you have been soaking in His presence. We cannot fake fruit. Eventually, whatever has been cultivated in secret will show up in public.

That is why the hidden seasons matter so much.

They shape the harvest.

Fruit Looks Like This

Paul described the fruit of the Spirit in *Galatians 5:22– 23:*

- Love
- Joy
- Peace
- Patience
- Kindness

- Goodness

- Faithfulness

- Gentleness

- Self-control

This isn't about perfection; it is about evidence. As you abide in Christ, these fruits begin to show up, not because you are striving, but because you are connected to the Vine.

> *"Remain in me, as I also remain in you. No branch can bear fruit by itself; it must remain in the vine." John 15:4 (NIV)*

The Harvest is for His Glory

This isn't about building a brand. It isn't about showing off your healing. It isn't about proving your worth. It is about glorifying the One who never left you in the dirt. Every fruit of healing, strength, wisdom, and compassion is a mirror that reflects Jesus.

> *"Let your light so shine before others, that they may see your good deeds and glorify your Father in heaven." Matthew 5:16 (NIV)*

He gets the glory. We get the joy of being part of it.

Harvest Doesn't Mean You Stop Growing

The harvest is beautiful, but it is not the end. It is only a glimpse of what God can do through a surrendered life. Each new season brings new soil, new stretching, and new fruit.

So, do not idolize the bloom. Stay surrendered to the Gardener.

Let Him prune again.

Let Him plant something new.

And, let Him continue multiplying what He started in you.

Reflection Questions

What fruit is my life currently producing—and what does it reveal about my roots?

Have I embraced the harvest season with humility and purpose?

Who is God calling me to nourish with the fruit from my story?

Prayer Prompt

Jesus,

Thank You for the harvest. Thank You for being faithful to bring fruit from every tear, every surrender, and every season in the soil. Let my life be evidence of Your goodness.

Let the fruit You have grown in me bring healing to others, and may it all point back to You.

Keep me connected to the Vine.

Keep me humble.

Keep me hungry for more of You.

In Your name, amen.

Chapter 7

Multiplying the Seed – Empowering Others

The fruit of your life is not the end goal. It is the beginning of someone else's healing.

The beauty of the Kingdom is that God never wastes a seed.

When you allow Him to plant you, prune you, and raise you, He doesn't just bless you. He multiplies through you.

What You Survive, You Can Steward

Your story carries weight. What you have walked through is not just for you; it is for the people God is calling you to reach. You do not need a platform. You do not need a microphone. You simply need a willing heart.

God uses broken vessels because they pour the most.

> *"They triumphed over him by the blood of the Lamb and by the word of their testimony..." Revelation 12:11 (NIV)*

Your testimony isn't just powerful. It is prophetic. When you share it, you take the shame off someone else.

When you testify, you give permission for someone else to rise.

Multiplication Comes Through Surrender

In *John 6*, a young boy brought his small lunch to Jesus: five loaves and two fish. It wasn't enough to feed the crowd, but it was surrendered. Jesus took what seemed insufficient and multiplied it. That is exactly what He does with your life. You do not have to be the most qualified. You do not have to have it all together. You simply have to bring Him what you have. When you surrender your testimony, your gifts, and your time, He multiplies it.

From Blooming to Bearing More

God didn't call you to simply bloom beautifully. He called you to reproduce spiritually; to be a seed carrier, to plant truth in others, and to speak life wherever you go.

To guide women out of the ground that once held you captive.

There is someone who doesn't yet know how to fight, how to forgive, or how to worship through pain. But you do.

There is someone stuck in shame, not knowing there is freedom on the other side of surrender. But you do.

And your obedience can be the key to their breakthrough.

It Doesn't Have to Be Big—Just Spirit- Led

Empowering others doesn't mean launching a ministry overnight.

It might look like:

- Praying with a friend who's barely holding on.
- Leading a small group or Bible study.
- Sending a voice note of encouragement.

- Testifying at a women's gathering.

- Creating a space for healing and worship Don't wait to be asked—start where you are.

- You've been equipped through your story. Now it's time to sow into someone else's.

There's More Seed in Your Hand

The beautiful thing about fruit is that it carries seed. Every breakthrough carries the potential to birth more.

Every healed place in your life now holds the authority to bring healing to others. You were never meant to keep it to yourself.

This is the multiplication season. The same God who brought you through the breaking will use your bloom to plant revival in someone else.

You Are a Carrier of Kingdom Seed

You are a vessel. You are an answer to someone's prayer. You are living evidence that God restores. You are a walking testimony of resurrection power.

So, go! Speak. Love.

Sow. Multiply what He has done in you.

Reflection Questions

Who around me needs the encouragement or wisdom I've gained from my journey?

What is one small step I can take to begin pouring into someone else?

Have I been hiding my story—or allowing God to use it for Kingdom multiplication?

Prayer Prompt

Jesus,

I don't want to just bear fruit; I want to multiply. Use my story to plant hope in others. Use my healing to bring healing. Use my yes to unlock someone else's.

Show me who You are calling me to encourage, empower, and equip.

Make me bold. Make me faithful.

And let every seed You have sown in me be sown again, for Your glory.

In Your name, amen.

Chapter 8

The Anatomy of a Seed
– What It Teaches Us
About Faith

Every seed has a story.

Before it becomes a plant, before it bears fruit, before anyone sees what it's becoming, it begins in obscurity: silent, small, hidden, covered by soil.
Just like our faith.

The Seed Coat – The Outer Shell

This is the part you see, the protective layer. It represents the parts of us that are still guarded: our flesh, our pride, our fear. These are the layers that keep us from going deeper.

Before a seed can grow, the coat must break. There's pressure in the soil. Moisture. Friction. All of it softens the outer layer until it finally cracks open.

> *"Unless a kernel of wheat falls to the ground and dies, it remains only a single seed..." (John 12:24, NIV)*

Sometimes the breaking feels like loss, but it's actually the beginning of transformation.

The Embryo – The Life Within

Inside every seed is a living core: the blueprint, the potential, the calling that's been placed by the Creator.

No one can see it from the outside, but it's there. This is your identity in Christ.

Your purpose. Your gifting. Your future.

Even when life looks dormant, God knows what's inside you.

The soil might feel suffocating, but the pressure is creating the perfect environment for what's been planted in you to grow.

The Endosperm – The Internal Nourishment

This is what feeds the seed until it has roots. In

spiritual terms, this is the Word of God. It's His promises. His presence.

It's the truths you return to when you can't see fruit yet.

God gives you what you need for the in-between, the waiting, the silent seasons.

Even in the dark places where you feel unseen, His Word continues to sustain you.

> *"Man shall not live by bread alone, but by every word that comes from the mouth of God." (Matthew 4:4, ESV)*

The Radicle – The First Root

This is the first visible sign of growth. It pushes downward before anything rises upward.

It may go unseen by others, but it is crucial for stability. This root determines how deep and strong the plant can become.

The radicle is your faith in action. It is your worship in the secret place, your midnight prayers, and your obedience when no one is watching.

It is underground growth—and it is everything.

The Shoot – Breaking the Surface

Eventually, after all the pressing, a tiny shoot pushes up through the soil.

It may not look like much, but it's proof that life is happening.

It's the breakthrough. The answered prayer. The open door.

But even then, growth continues, because this is only the beginning of what God is building in you.

What the Seed Teaches Us About Faith

Faith starts small – You don't need a forest, just a seed.

Faith grows in silence – Don't despise the still seasons.

Faith must break before it multiplies, the shell can't stay intact.

Faith is nourished by truth; stay grounded in the Word.

Faith leads to the fruit we enrich in ourselves, but only through surrender.

You Were Never Buried to Die—You Were Planted to Rise

The enemy wants you to believe that the darkness means it's over. But the soil is not your grave; it is your greenhouse.

God is growing you in places others cannot see.

And when the time is right, you will rise.

The seed was never the final form. It was only the beginning.

Conclusion

Final Commissioning Word

You've been through the soil. You've endured the breaking.

You've worshiped through silence.

You've clung to truth when nothing made sense. And now, it's time to bloom.

But this bloom isn't just for you. It's for the Kingdom.

It's for the people waiting on the other side of your obedience.

It's for every woman who still feels buried and doesn't know that resurrection is coming.

You Are Commissioned

You are not just a survivor. You are a seed carrier.

A messenger.

A forerunner.

Your life is prophetic evidence that God restores, heals, rebuilds, and multiplies.

You've been hidden, but not forgotten. You've been pruned, but not punished.

You've been broken, but not discarded. And now, God is calling you to rise.

You Are Called to Bear Fruit That Remains

> "You did not choose me, but I chose you
> and appointed you so that you might go
> and bear fruit—fruit that will last..."
> *John 15:16 (NIV)*

The fruit God produces through your life will nourish others.

Your story will break chains.

Your healing will activate healing.

Your surrender will unlock revival.

Your worship will shift atmospheres.

Don't hold back.

You are not too young, too late, too wounded, or too small.

You are anointed. You are appointed.

You are commissioned by Heaven to bloom and multiply for His glory.

Go Plant What He's Grown in You

This isn't the end of your story—it's the beginning of your legacy.

So, rise, daughter.

Speak, daughter.

Go, daughter.

And may the seeds you sow in others bloom for generations to come.

Faith Declaration Prayer

I declare…

I am not buried; I am planted.

God is growing something beautiful in me, even in the dark.

I may not see fruit yet, but I trust the process.

I believe…

God is faithful to complete the good work He began in me.

What the enemy meant for harm, God is turning for good.

My life will bear fruit that glorifies Him and nourishes others.

I declare…

My past does not disqualify me.

My pain will produce purpose. My story will break chains.

I believe…

I am a daughter of the Most High God—chosen, set apart, and deeply loved.

The same power that raised Christ from the dead lives in me.

I am rooted in truth, equipped by the Word, and led by the Spirit.

I declare…

I am not too late.

I am not too broken. I am not forgotten.

I believe…

This is my bloom season. This is my moment to rise.

This is my time to walk in purpose and multiply what God has planted in me.

In Jesus' name, Amen.

Faith Seeds to Hide in Your Heart

These are the scriptures that carried me through the soil. When you feel buried, broken, or forgotten, hide these in your heart. Speak them out loud. Declare them over your dry places. Let them water your faith when nothing else makes sense.

You weren't buried to die. You were planted to rise.

When You Feel Buried or Forgotten

> *"The Lord will guide you always; He will satisfy your needs in a sun-scorched land and will strengthen your frame..." Isaiah 58:11*

> *"I will give you a new heart and put a new spirit in you..." Ezekiel 36:26*

> *"Though I sit in darkness, the Lord will be my light." Micah 7:8*

When You're in a Season of Breaking

> *"Unless a kernel of wheat falls to the ground and dies, it remains only a single seed. But if it dies, it produces many seeds." John 12:24*

> *"He heals the brokenhearted and binds up their wounds." Psalm 147:3*

"You have recorded my troubles. You have kept a list of my tears." Psalm 56:8 (CEV)

When God Is Pruning You for Purpose

"Every branch that does bear fruit He prunes so that it will be even more fruitful." John 15:2

"Humble yourselves… under God's mighty hand, that He may lift you up in due time." 1 Peter 5:6

"Consider it pure joy… whenever you face trials… because… the testing of your faith produces perseverance." James 1:2–3

When You're Learning to Trust His Voice

"My sheep hear My voice, and I know them, and they follow Me." John 10:27

"Your word is a lamp to my feet and a light to my path." Psalm 119:105

"In returning and rest you shall be saved; in quietness and in trust shall

be your strength." Isaiah 30:15 (ESV)

When You Need Strength to Obey

"Trust in the Lord with all your heart and lean not on your own understanding." Proverbs 3:5–6

"Blessed are those who hear the word of God and obey it." Luke 11:28

"If you are willing and obedient, you shall eat the good of the land." Isaiah 1:19

When You're Waiting for Fruit to Bloom

"Those who sow with tears will reap with songs of joy." Psalm 126:5

"Let us not become weary in doing good, for at the proper time we will reap a harvest..." Galatians 6:9

"Remain in Me, as I also remain in you. No branch can bear fruit by itself..." John 15:4

When You're Ready to Multiply What God Planted

> *"You did not choose Me, but I chose you and appointed you so that you might go and bear fruit—fruit that will last." John 15:16*

> *"They overcame him by the blood of the Lamb and by the word of their testimony…" Revelation 12:11*

> *"The Spirit of the Sovereign Lord is upon me… to bind up the brokenhearted… to proclaim freedom… to comfort all who mourn." Isaiah 61:1–2*

Let these verses anchor you.

Speak them when you feel shaky. Write them down.

Declare them over your children, your future, and your buried places.

Faith doesn't grow by accident; it grows when the

Word is watered.

So, water it.

Speak it.

Hide it in your heart.

You are rooted in truth.

You are anchored in grace.

You are growing, even here.

The end.

About the Author

Vanessa Ortiz is a worshiper, intercessor, Christian athlete, mentor, and woman of faith who has walked through seasons of breaking, hiddenness, and divine transformation. Known for her transparency, spiritual wisdom, and gentle authority, Vanessa carries an anointing to lead others from pain to purpose through the power of Jesus Christ.

A single mother of two beautiful children, Vanessa's life is a living testimony of God's healing, restoration, and unfailing grace.

Her heart beats for helping women discover their identity in Christ, hear God's voice clearly, and bloom into their God-given calling, no matter how buried they may feel.

She ministers through movement, worship, and prophetic intercession, and has been marked by the Holy Spirit to equip others for healing and breakthrough.

Buried to Bloom is her debut book, a Spirit-led offering born from the soil of personal struggle and supernatural growth.

Vanessa desires to see women rise in faith, walk in obedience, and bloom fully for His glory.

Connect with Vanessa

For speaking engagements or mentoring, please contact:

vortiz1410@gmail.com

Dear Reader,

Thank you from the bottom of my heart for taking the time to read this book. It is my prayer that these words touched your spirit, offered encouragement, and brought clarity or hope into your life.

Whether you are at the beginning of your journey or deep in the trenches of transformation, know that you are not alone—God walks with you every step of the way.

Writing this book was a calling and a labor of love. I poured my heart, faith, and experiences into every page, trusting that even one sentence could spark change or offer comfort to someone in need.

If something within these pages inspired you, helped you grow, or gave you a deeper understanding of your purpose, I give God all the glory.

If you found value in this book, I humbly ask you to leave an honest review on Amazon and Goodreads. Your feedback not only helps others discover this message, but also strengthens the community of faith and encouragement that we're building together.

Vanessa Ortiz

May God bless you, guide you, and continue to light your path.

With gratitude and grace,

Vanessa

www.ingramcontent.com/pod-product-compliance
Lightning Source LLC
LaVergne TN
LVHW051809080426
835513LV00017B/1885